D0324186

Written by Woody Guthrie
Illustrated by Vera Rosenberry

Good Year Books

I'm going to wrap myself in paper.

I'm going to dab myself with glue.

Stick some stamps
on top of my head.

I'm going to mail myself to you.

I'm going to tie me up
in red string.

I'm going to tie blue ribbons, too.

I'm going to climb up in my
mailbox. I'm going to mail
myself to you.